A LITTLE GUIDE TO A BIG LIFE

A LITTLE GUIDE TO A BIG LIFE

DAVID YOUNG

Wind Runner Press
Round Rock, Texas

Introduction

I struggled to find the right adjective for *life. Successful, rewarding,* and *happy* are a few of the better ones that came to mind, but even these are inadequate. Life is just too big.

Big. That's the adjective I was looking for.

I discovered after I had been married several years that my life wasn't big, it was just busy.

"You used to smile whenever you saw me," my wife, Christina, reminded me. "That made me feel special. But you don't smile when you see me anymore, and I miss that."

My love for Christina had grown, and she still turned heads, especially mine, so I had lots of reasons to smile. But she was right. I didn't smile as often as I used to, because I was usually thinking about my to-do list. I appreciated her gentle reminder. I made a few changes and started smiling again. We're both happier now.

In this little guide I share what I've learned about life, in the form of gentle reminders. You probably already know how to live a big life. If so, you don't need a big book. But perhaps some reminders would help you too.

There are extra pages in the back you can use to add reminders for yourself or, if this book is a gift for someone, to share thoughts that have been meaningful to you over the years.

Gentle Reminder #1: Smile when you see your spouse.

No one is too small to make a difference. Just ask Goliath.

~

Tie your identity to who you are, such as cheerful and honest, not to what you do, such as sell real estate.

Have fun every day. You'll lose part of yourself if you're serious all the time.

Take your children for walks. They'll remember them long after you're gone.

~

Work for the salary you want, not the salary you get.

~

The wrong way to avoid making a big mistake is to do nothing. The right way is to move forward, making small mistakes along the way and learning from them.

~

Losers who stay losers look back. Losers who become winners look forward.

Don't lecture your spouse when he or she makes a mistake. Hug and forgive.

Be willing to pay a little extra for good customer service.
You'll save yourself a lot of headaches.

~

Give advice by asking questions that will lead the other
person to the right answer.

Laughter changes your focus from the pain of the past to the hope of the future.

Your time away from the spotlight is important because that's when your character is tested and developed. Anyone can do the right thing in public, but it takes a person of integrity to do the right thing when no one is watching.

~

The world is telling the people you love that they're only as good as their last performance review. Remind them often that you love them unconditionally.

~

You have the power to make a difference where you are right now. Don't waste it by dreaming about another time and place.

~

Don't judge each day by your accomplishments, because you may not see immediate results. Instead, judge it by your commitment to your long-term plan.

It's hard to learn with your mouth open. Listen and you'll become wise.

Don't judge others by their looks. Successful people come in all shapes and sizes.

~

Strong people admit when they're wrong, and they're silent when they're right.

~

Share armrests.

Don't focus on your weaknesses. They'll pull you back. Focus instead on your strengths. They'll pull you forward.

~

Always have positive things to say and people will look forward to talking to you.

~

Apologize quickly. Long battles are costly.

~

Take the time you spend judging, criticizing, talking about, and advising others, and use it to improve yourself.

~

Don't be controlled by circumstances. Instead, set goals, make plans, and fight for what you want.

Family members usually ask you to do things with them at the most inconvenient times. Do them anyway.

Children give you an excuse to live again: to slow down, to sing silly songs, to chase fireflies, to build snowmen, and to soar on park swings. They keep your spirit young and your heart full of love. No success brings as much joy as being with children.

A budget gives you the courage to spend wisely so you can live freely.

~

People who do the most good often do it under the worst circumstances.

~

Confident people aren't free of failure. They're just free of the fear of failure.

~

Never be deceived into thinking that a choice between right and wrong is insignificant. Every act shapes your character.

A Little Guide to a Big Life

Don't answer the phone when you're eating with your family.

~

Great people treat others as equals.

~

Every job is important if it provides a product or service people need.

~

Losing is temporary, but quitting is forever.

Time flies for you, but it moves slowly for your children, especially when you're gone. Their day is like an eternity. Spend as many eternities with them as possible.

You'll spend more time climbing the mountain than standing on the summit, so enjoy the journey.

～

People who have suffered know how to help those who are suffering.

～

Perfect jobs are a myth, so don't be discouraged if you don't like some aspects of yours. Focus on what you enjoy and the other parts won't seem as onerous.

Water relationships with kindness and watch them blossom.

~

You'll find happy people in hospitals, slums, and war zones, and unhappy people in mansions, five-star restaurants, and country clubs. It's not what you have. It's what you appreciate.

~

God uses imperfect people who are in imperfect situations to do His perfect will.

~

Forgive people, even when they don't apologize.

You can't raise happy, healthy kids if you aren't happy and healthy. Set aside time for yourself every day, regardless of how busy you are. This will help you keep a good attitude and preserve the strength necessary for the long run. Raising kids is a marathon, not a sprint.

People waiting for big opportunities are passed by people taking advantage of small ones.

Anger gives you bad advice.

~

Impact people. Don't impress them. People who impress help only when they can showcase their talents. People who impact help regardless of the task, even if it's just to sweep and mop.

Dust off your blessings and you'll find happiness.

~

Focus on what's important, not on what's urgent. We respond to crises quickly because we want them to go away. But we can get so distracted by them that we don't take care of our priorities, such as our family and health, until they become crises. By then, it may be too late.

~

There are no dead ends, only opportunities to change directions.

~

Many successful people started with nothing. So if you have nothing, you have everything you need to succeed.

~

Goals help you survive tough times because they give you something to look forward to.

~

Take charge of your career. If it's slipped, don't blame it on your boss or coworkers. Become indispensable by updating your skills, volunteering for projects, and going the extra mile. Make your boss and coworkers look good, and they'll make you look good.

Detours can be blessings. Dusty roads take you to interesting places.

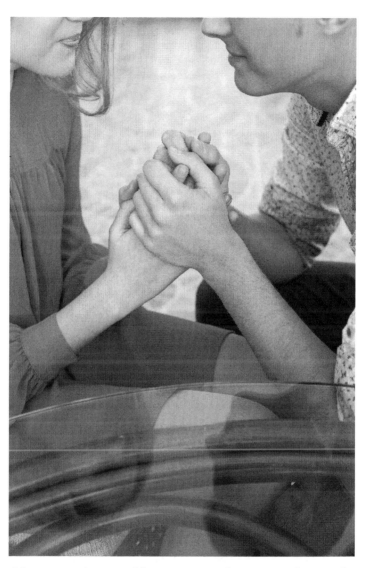

Many marriage problems start with a misunderstanding. When there's friction, deal with it quickly. Ask your spouse how you offended him or her. Then ask for forgiveness.

Not everything that enters your mind should exit your lips.

You can hold your children closer with your ears than with your arms, so listen patiently.

~

People who accomplished big things did a lot of small things first.

~

Find a cause so important you'll pursue it regardless of the obstacles.

~

Victims have problems; victors have solutions. Victims have hurts; victors have forgiveness. Victims have shattered dreams; victors have new dreams.

Learn to be an expert by first learning to be a beginner.

~

When adversity disrupts your routine, you may find new meaning and happiness.

~

Do ordinary things extraordinarily well and you'll stand out.

~

Slowing down to 10 MPH as you approach a green light, just in case it turns red, is a self-fulfilling prophecy. Move confidently through life. Expect the best instead of the worst.

The person God made you to be is better than the person others think you should be.

~

Happiness is a balloon that pops when circumstances change. But joy is an inner peace that withstands anything.

~

Smile as if you were the most beautiful person in the world. It will make you feel and look beautiful.

~

Change is painful, which is why we'd rather change others than ourselves. But if we can't change ourselves, then we probably can't change others either.

Tell your friends often why they're dear to you.

People who persevere learn from their mistakes. People who give up never learn.

~

When you have a problem with someone you love, look for a solution, not an exit.

~

The earth, sun, moon, and stars are marvelous creations, but not as marvelous as you.

~

You become the person you imagine yourself to be.

~

When you're playing, don't think about work, and when you're working, don't think about play.

~

The biggest obstacle falls when you take the first step.

~

People who base their identity on what they do are more likely to do things they shouldn't to get ahead than people who base their identity on who they are.

Leaders who crave approval are actually followers.

Keep your pantry stocked with popcorn.

The welfare of mankind is more dependent on the small acts of humble people who are in unseen places than the heroic deeds of leaders who are in the spotlight.

Don't let obstacles stop you. They're often smaller than they appear, and you're stronger than you realize.

～

Invest so much in achieving your goals that the pain of quitting would be more than the pain of persevering.

～

Honor your company, boss, and coworkers, and others will want you on their team.

～

How you treat the cashier after you've waited in a long line says a lot about your character.

A boy has been described as a noise with some dirt on it. Make sure some of the dirt is from sweeping and some of the noise is from vacuuming. It's easier for kids to start good habits, such as doing chores, before they start elementary school than when they're teenagers.

~

A raised voice makes a weak point.

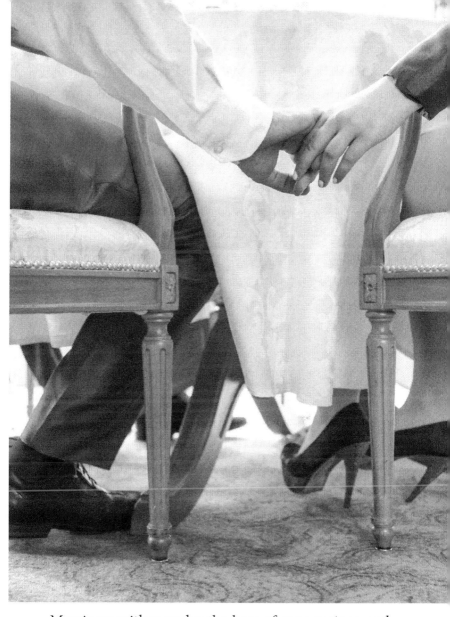

Marriages wither under the heat of expectations and criticism, but flourish under the rain of encouragement and praise.

Stay young by learning new things.

~

The ability to endure drudgery separates winners from losers.

~

Life is more fun when you tackle tough challenges.

~

God gave everyone unique qualities that make them beautiful, but some people cover their beauty with a negative attitude, because they don't like the way they look. Uncover your beauty by finding things you like about yourself.

Ride the merry-go-round at the fall carnival.

Start the day by reading something inspirational.

The annoying noise your children make today will be the noise you'll miss when they're grown and gone.

~

Set aside money each paycheck for your next car so you can pay cash.

Happiness isn't at the end of the road. It's under your feet.

Do small jobs well and you'll be recruited for bigger jobs.

~

Adversity reminds you to be grateful for the things you've taken for granted.

~

Expect criticism when you're doing good. Few things are accomplished without it.

~

Prepare your children for independence by weaning them off of reminders and lectures. They'll make mistakes, but they'll get better, if you allow them to suffer the consequences. Kids forget warnings, but they remember pain.

Learn about the Creator by examining His creation. The beauty and perfection of a white orchid, the power of the sun, the grandeur of the stars, and the unconditional love of a Labrador retriever, all reflect God.

~

Do the unpleasant duties first and you'll enjoy the rest of the day.

Everyone likes a good listener.

Do big things for your wife and you'll get her attention.
Do little things for her and you'll get her heart.

Kill giants with whatever God has given you, even if it's just a slingshot and five smooth stones.

~

Don't let your net worth determine your self-worth. Who you are is more important than what you have.

~

Sometimes the room has to be darkened by adversity before you can discover other sources of light.

~

Not everyone can succeed with talent, but everyone can succeed with hard work.

You'll delay many things when you have kids: vacations, major purchases, nights out with friends – and old age. You'll dress younger, think younger, be more active, take better care of yourself, and have more to look forward to, such as time with your children and grandchildren.

$\sim$

The fear of failure stops progress. Failure only slows it.

$\sim$

Tell people they're great, and they'll prove you're right.

$\sim$

Start with the assumption that your spouse is right. Look at things from his or her perspective.

Confident people know their efforts will pay off, so they're patient.

Listen to music at night. It will clear your mind and help you sleep.

When you tell your boss about a problem, offer a solution.

~

No one is good at everything, but everyone is good at something. Celebrate the things you're good at, and don't worry about the rest.

~

When you don't have what you need, you become creative with what you have.

~

Enjoy the slow moments. If you're only happy during big events, then you'll be unhappy most of the time.

~

When you're in an argument, don't try to win. Try to restore unity.

~

Maintain your character, regardless of the cost. It's your most valuable asset.

~

When you reach your financial goals, you'll barely remember the things you gave up to achieve them.

Travel, read, enjoy the arts, and play sports. You'll meet interesting people, and you'll become an interesting person.

Let teens wash your car when they're raising money for their church or school.

~

Give your children clear boundaries and enforce them. Boundaries allow them to control the outcomes, because they know what the outcomes will be before they act. This makes them feel secure.

A house full of family and friends is more beautiful than a house full of fine furnishings.

~

The best thing you'll discover on an adventure is yourself.

~

Listen to the birds sing when you're outside.

~

Reliable people find favor with others.

~

The price of money is too high if it costs you the love and companionship of your spouse and children, your health, or your integrity.

Adversity brings out your best. Heroes emerge during a crisis.

~

Avoid embarrassment and hurt feelings by talking about others as if they were present.

~

Tell people how they've impacted your life. They'll be blessed to know you appreciate them.

~

Successful people pursue their dreams despite the obstacles, hard work, and slow results.

A Little Guide to a Big Life

The thief who steals your family time takes your most valuable possession.

Everyone, regardless of their social status, knows something you don't know and has had experiences you haven't had. Learn from them.

~

People striving for excellence pass those striving for greatness.

~

When people are selfish, ungrateful, or mean, love them anyway.

~

Be humble, and wise people will share their wisdom with you.

~

The six most powerful words are, "I was wrong. Please forgive me."

~

Failure frees you from the fear of failure, because you learn it isn't fatal.

~

Visualize success, regardless of the circumstances.

Fill your children with good thoughts before they go to bed. Ask them about their favorite part of the day, praise them for a good deed, pray with them, and tell them they're the best gift God ever gave you. They'll fall asleep feeling ten feet tall.

Live as if you had lost everything and then suddenly got it all back.

~

Smile. You'll appear confident and friendly, and people will want to meet you.

~

Don't rush people who are ahead of you, especially if they're elderly.

~

Smart people share what they know. Wise people learn what others know.

~

If you have to choose between a job you love and a job that pays the bills, do the latter. But if you can choose between two jobs that pay the bills, do what you enjoy most, even if it pays less. If you love your job, you'll put your heart into it and do it well, which will bring honor to yourself and your profession.

~

Problems are blessings in disguise. They teach you to be creative, stretch your comfort zone, and force you to develop new relationships.

Successful people keep their youthful charm. They're spontaneous, bold, lovers of wit, and travelers.

Don't make decisions when you're discouraged, tired, angry, or pressured to decide quickly.

~

Character is your foundation. Make it strong and you'll stand when others fall.

~

Remove the clutter from your desk. You may look busy when it's messy, but you aren't paid to look busy, or even to be busy. You're paid to be productive.

~

Tell young people the good character and personality traits you see in them. You'll boost their confidence.

~

Treat everyone at work as if they were the president of the company.

~

If marriage doesn't end your selfishness, your selfishness will end your marriage.

~

When anger grows, beauty fades.

Work with so much enthusiasm that people stop to watch.

~

Leaders take the initiative to get to know others.

~

Break your goals into small steps you can take every day, so they won't overwhelm you. Think big, but start small.

You can be as happy buying groceries as you can buying diamonds, as happy writing a letter to a friend as you can writing a best-selling novel, and as happy teaching your children as you can teaching law students at Harvard – if you do these with gratitude for what you have and what you can give.

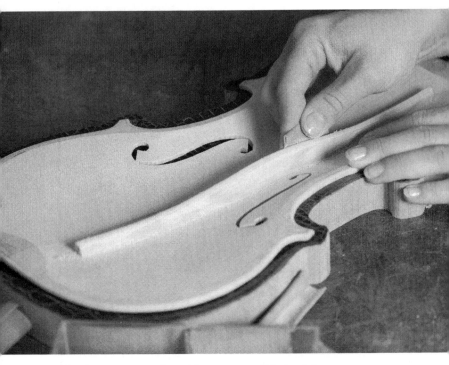

God gave you talent. You must add the labor.

~

The things you do first always get done.

~

What you do when things get hard says a lot about you.

~

The best way to end an argument is to admit you were wrong. Humility resolves more conflicts than reason.

Let your children play with the box the refrigerator came in, push the shopping cart, tell you knock-knock jokes, and hold your hand when you walk. Simple pleasures are better than expensive gifts.

~

People who are asked to do the impossible often do it.

~

Wisdom is realizing that what you got is better than what you wanted.

Beautiful people don't always enjoy life, but people who enjoy life are always beautiful.

~

Teach your children about money by sharing your financial goals with them, and by showing them how you achieve them.

~

The secret to happiness is to spend more time thinking about others and less time thinking about yourself.

Don't put off leisure until you retire. You may not live that long.

~

The joy of getting something new quickly turns into the boredom of having something old. Restore your joy by giving.

~

Money is a poor substitute for happiness. Don't let it lure you into the wrong career.

~

You increase your self-esteem every time you follow through on a commitment.

Perseverance unlocks doors Genius can't.

Goals work on you while you work on them.

~

It's been said that as soon as we can afford a fishing rod, we buy a fishing boat. If you want to live like a million- aire, save like a millionaire. Spend below your means and invest the difference.

~

A closed door forces you to try another door, which you may like better.

~

Never stop learning. What you learn after you think you know enough will change your life.

~

Get advice on big decisions. You may be so tangled in the details that you can't see the big picture.

~

What you say about others says a lot about you.

~

People who overcome difficulties are compassionate, which makes them beautiful.

Don't be discouraged by humble beginnings. All big things started small.

~

Help others with a kind act, not a wise word.

~

God won't show you the second step until you've taken the first.

~

Character is a friend who reassures you during adversity that you'll triumph if you keep doing the right thing.

God made you the way you are because the world needs your unique strengths. Don't deprive others of your talents by trying to be like someone else.

Do something every day that will surprise and please your spouse.

~

All service pleases God, regardless of the giver's talent.

~

Hold people tightly and things loosely.

~

Be the bigger person and apologize first.

~

Every great artist has a closet full of bad paintings.

Be the first to hug and the last to let go.

Before you have children, you imagine the happiness they'll bring. When you have them, the reality sinks in: they require a lot of time, work, and money. It's not always fun. When they're grown, you realize they brought you more happiness than you ever thought possible.

~

Don't give up when you do your best but fail. You can't control the circumstances, but you can control your effort. Continue to work hard, and look for ways to improve. If the door stays closed, your effort will reveal new opportunities.

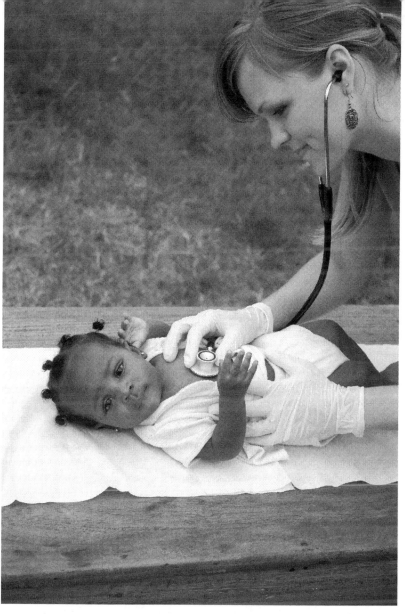

Live so that if your life were cut short, it could be said that its width made up for its length.

Initiate conversations with others. Some of them will become your dear friends.

~

Adversity makes you realize that the beauty inside you is greater than the beauty around you.

~

Money won't make you happy. It'll just make you want more money.

~

In a disagreement, make your point respectfully. You won't embarrass yourself if you're wrong, or the other person if you're right.

When you feel lifeless, go somewhere that's full of life, such as a garden, a park, or the zoo.

~

Maintain a cash reserve equal to three months of your income for major repairs, illnesses, layoffs, and other emergencies.

~

Average people focus on people's faults, which helps them feel good about themselves. Superior people focus on people's strengths, which motivates them to improve.

Tall kids (people who are young at heart) set big goals, take risks, go on adventures, and stay flexible.

Be grateful for each day and enjoy the blessings it brings.

~

Passion contributes more to success than talent.

~

If you do everything your boss asks, then you're an average employee, and you'll get average pay. To earn a raise and a promotion, do more than your boss asks.

~

Don't say things about others that would hurt them, even if they're true.

~

If you don't start the day knowing what you're going to do, you'll end it wondering what you did.

~

Successful people adjust quickly when they make a mistake, and they keep going.

~

Pity those who have good looks but lack beauty. Youth fades, but integrity, courage, discipline, and love – which are the true marks of beauty – never do.

Dump your long-term plan to find happiness. Be happy today.

A forever marriage requires a forgiving couple.

~

Decide every morning to find something good in every-one you meet and in every situation you encounter.

~

Honor others with your full attention when they're talking. Don't interrupt, tap your fingers, look around the room, or finish their sentences for them.

~

Three great exercises are push-ups, sit-ups, and setbacks. The first two build your body. The last one builds your character.

Go to church with your mother on Mother's Day.

~

Give liberally to your spouse without measuring, and receive gratefully without measuring. Marriages treated like business transactions sour quickly.

Spend as much time maximizing your children's potential as you do minimizing their problems. Smile when they come into the room, listen when they talk, hug them when they tell the truth, and tell them you're proud of them when they do their best, regardless of the outcome.

Become the person you want to be by doing the things that person would do. To become wise, read; to become brave, do things outside your comfort zone; to become well-liked, introduce yourself to new people.

Return things you borrow promptly.

~

Adversity at the bottom prepares you for success at the top.

~

Everything is either a blessing or something you can turn into a blessing by learning from it.

~

It's easy to find unhappy people who have received much. It's hard to find unhappy people who have given much.

~

Don't focus on material success. It has a short life, because it's affected by forces beyond your control, such as the economy. Instead, focus on personal success, which can never be taken away. Create personal success by doing quality work, developing strong relationships, maintaining joy, and having a positive attitude.

~

Multiply the price of each item by two to determine its true cost. A $1 item costs approximately $2 in earnings, when you account for taxes (income, Social Security, Medicare, and sales).

Weight training is good, but wait training is better.
Patience overcomes more obstacles than power.

Sing along, even if you don't have a good voice.

~

Upgrade the status of your job by doing it so well others will want to do what you're doing.

~

Love people when they don't deserve it. That's when they need it most.

~

Don't wait for good things to knock on your door. Go knock on their doors.

~

The greatest tragedy of putting off spending time with your wife isn't the lost day, it's the fact that you decided that something else was more important, and that one day can easily turn into years.

If you're certain you can do the work, perhaps you aren't thinking big enough. Look for a job that will put you outside your comfort zone. This is the only way to grow.

Give your children responsibilities. The successful completion of small tasks will build their confidence and make them want to do bigger ones.

~

We search for truth when life gets uncomfortable.

~

Unsuccessful people use obstacles as an excuse to quit. Successful people use them to learn new skills.

~

If you see the strengths of others, but not your own, take on new challenges. You'll surprise yourself with what you can do.

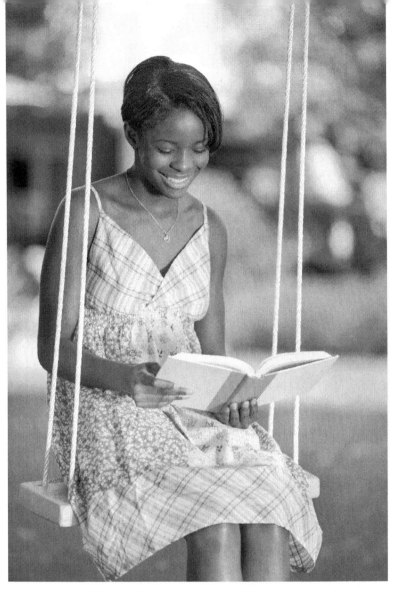

Expert problem solvers are creative. They connect things in new ways, and they have lots of experiences to connect. Improve your problem solving skills by visiting new places, broadening your reading list, and talking to others about their interests.

Park in the middle of one space and you'll decrease the number of four-letter words used by others who are trying to park.

Happiness doesn't come from good fortune. It comes from a good attitude.

Pet a dog when you're sad.

~

Stay confident when you make a mistake. No one is perfect.

~

Your wounds won't heal until you forgive.

~

Seeds sown during hard times yield rich harvests.

Try something new today. If you enjoy it, then you can enjoy it for the rest of your life.

Servants attract people and become leaders.

~

Success isn't moving big obstacles, but making big obstacles moveable by breaking them into small pieces.

~

Don't add an activity until you've eliminated one.

~

God is more than our rewarder. He is our reward.

~

Failures attribute success to talent and luck. Successful people attribute it to hard work.

~

The pain of loss is healed by the joy of giving.

~

Set goals, but don't put off happiness until you achieve them.

~

Always act like a winner.

Make smiley faces on your pancakes with fruit toppings.

~

Keep your word, even if the circumstances have changed since you gave it.

~

Don't reach for the potato chips when you're stressed or anxious. Exercise instead. It'll relieve tension, and you won't feel guilty about adding calories.

~

Work as if you were the one paying your salary.

Tell your children you love them and your life wouldn't be the same without them, even when they're adults.

~

When life seems unfair, visit someone in a prison, a hospital, or an orphanage. Your problems will seem small in comparison.

Be kind to everyone. You never know who is hurting and would be encouraged by your good deed.

Fly a kite. It'll remind you to set your sights high.

A Little Guide to a Big Life

Don't just ask your children at the end of the day what they did, participate in their activities. Play with them, help them with their homework, and get to know their friends. Let them know you think they're wonderful, and you can't resist spending time with them.

Don't be afraid of the unknown. Life gets bigger with each adventure.

~

People who are content with God's provisions have less debt.

~

Live the way you want your children to live. If you want them to control their tempers, then control yours. Telling them how to behave won't work if your actions don't match your words.

~

Good character is developed during bad times.

If you enjoy the journey, become a better person along the way, and help others, you'll be successful, regardless of how far you travel.

Don't wait for inspiration. You often generate your best ideas while you work.

~

Successful people are willing to look foolish while they learn new things.

~

Don't compare your success with anyone else's. You're an apple; they're an orange.

~

Don't envy what others have unless you want their problems too.

~

Do something so difficult you become a better person in the process.

~

Excess is keeping much for yourself. Success is giving much to others.

~

Don't get a laugh at someone else's expense. It's okay to make fun of yourself, but not others.

A life-lift will slow the aging process more than a face-lift. Raise your expectations, try new things, hang out with young people occasionally, and update your clothes.

~

Bring attention to the accomplishments of others.

~

Learn three interesting things about everyone you meet.

The most beautiful woman has kind lips, giving hands, and a loving heart.

The things you felt incapable of doing but you did anyway, the times you wanted to give up but you didn't, and the failures you rebounded from, have made you strong and capable of great things.

Tell your children often that you're proud of them, and tell them why.

~

When you see someone making a balloon animal, stop and watch.

~

Many successful people got their start in low-paying jobs doing high-quality work.

~

Don't underestimate yourself. You have more strengths than you realize, and your weaknesses won't limit you as much as you think.

Show as much excitement when you arrive at work as when you leave.

Love gives without measuring.

~

Everyone has handicaps. The greatest handicap is to have had nothing to overcome.

~

Making more money won't make you financially secure, but saving more money will.

~

Associate with great people. Small people want to bring you down to their level. Great people want to raise you above theirs.

~

Every obstacle has a weakness. When you get close, you'll see where to attack.

~

Successful people take calculated risks. When they fail, they keep working hard, and they recover.

~

God's power within you is greater than any power around you.

The secret to a happy marriage isn't eliminating differences, but eliminating resentment when differences keep you from getting what you want.

~

Your work is a reflection of you, so do it well, even if you'd rather be doing something else.

~

Many people who suddenly lost a family member had planned on spending more time with them when things slowed down.

Set goals that seem impossible and you'll achieve more than you thought possible.

A Little Guide to a Big Life

Wake up with enthusiasm and you'll go to bed with satisfaction.

Words spilled when angry are hard to clean up.

~

Don't give your children authority until they submit to yours.

~

Don't wait to start until you have all the answers. Some won't be revealed until you're on your way.

~

Worry is counterproductive because it saps the time and energy needed to solve problems.

~

When you're underutilized, be humble, teachable, and patient, and do your best work. Your attitude and performance will be rewarded.

~

Half of wisdom is getting advice. The other half is disregarding some of it.

~

The pleasure of possessions is short, but the burden of their debt is long.

No one is poor who has a good friend.

Good fathers take their sons fishing. Great fathers take their daughters too.

Genius can start a fire without wood, but it'll go out quickly. Wisdom collects the wood first.

Write love notes to your spouse.

∼

Don't be ashamed of failure. Be ashamed of not trying.

∼

Don't think about the offense after you forgive someone.

∼

A prideful person has only one admirer.

∼

Listening builds trust, which is why people open up when you listen.

Good fortune can disappear as quickly as it appears. But character, which is built decision by decision, like a stone fortress, will endure.

God gives you visions primarily so you can grow, so measure your success by what you become, not by what you achieve.

~

Don't try to fix your spouse unless you want your spouse to fix you.

~

Hire a neighborhood kid to mow your yard when you're out of town.

~

When you're discouraged about how far you have to go, look at how far you've already come.

~

Don't sit in the same section at church every Sunday. Get to know new people.

~

Borrowing money lowers your standard of living. The more you pay in interest, the less you have for other things.

Common things, such as a child's smile, a colorful sunset, or a friend's embrace, are priceless. Uncommon things, such as diamonds and gold, are merely high priced.

Treat your enemies well and they may become your allies.

~

In the first few years of your career, what you learn is more important than what you earn.

~

Don't argue so well that no one wants to talk to you.

~

You can't change the way people act, but you can change the way you react.

~

Admit when you're wrong. You'll gain credibility.

~

Winners persevere when they're losing.

~

The people you help will tell your story when you're gone.

~

Successful people start now. Failures wait for better circumstances.

A Little Guide to a Big Life

You can't catch happiness. It has to catch you. Slow down so it has an easy target.

∼

Stand up straight and you'll look confident and successful.

∼

You're irresistible to God. He delights in seeing you, He's always thinking about you, and He can't wait to hear your voice. You're one of His favorite creations.

∼

Love that starts as a feeling must be sustained by actions. If you don't feel in love anymore, show love, and the feelings will return.

Light up every room you enter with a smile.

Grow mentally by tackling problems that make you doubt your intelligence.

Greatness is developed when no one believes in you.

Find something every day for each of your senses to enjoy. Watch a kitten play with a ball of yarn. Listen to a bird sing. Smell a flower. Taste a cold melon. Touch a baby's cheek.

~

Successful people pursue their goals after the excitement of setting them has worn off.

Instead of worrying about your children's weaknesses, help them develop and use their strengths. This will give them the confidence to succeed, regardless of their weaknesses.

～

It's been said that the two happiest days in a man's life are the day he buys a boat and the day he sells it. Possessions often bring more headaches than happiness.

～

It's better to give 100 percent and lose than 90 percent and win. Less than full effort may bring short-term success, but long-term success requires full effort.

～

Staying busy may deaden the pain of unhappiness, but it won't fulfill you. Determine your purpose and use your time to fulfill it.

～

Set boundaries for your children. They want freedom to do as they please, but they also want to be safe. Tell them yes, and they may like you for the moment, but they'll distrust you later when they get hurt. Tell them no, and they may dislike you for the moment, but they'll get over it quickly, because they know you love them.

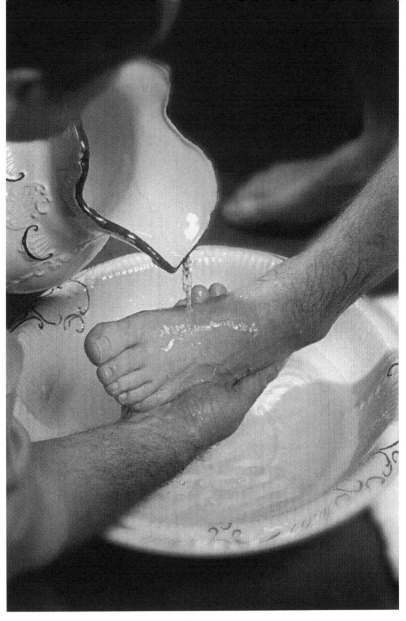

Don't judge yourself according to how your neighbors live, or you'll become complacent. Judge yourself according to how Jesus lived.

You are superior to adversity. You're smarter, faster, and more flexible. Persevere and you'll overcome it.

~

Don't just earn a paycheck. Earn a reputation for integrity, dependability, and excellence too.

~

If you focus on what you don't have, you won't do much with what you do have.

~

Don't try to change others so they'll be like you. It's the differences that make life interesting.

The shape of life changes as we age, but not its size – it's always big. It starts out long and narrow and ends up short and wide. Enjoy its breadth by discovering new places, hobbies, and music, and by rediscovering the places, hobbies, and music you enjoyed when you were young.

Encourage others to talk about themselves.

~

When you're hurting, help someone else. You'll both feel better.

~

The person who makes you angry controls your happiness.

~

Life swings open on the hinges of small deeds.

~

God uses the crippled hands of a person whose heart is yielded to Him.

~

Successful people take advantage of imperfect opportunities others refuse.

~

Don't take on more than you can do calmly.

~

Great people act boldly but speak humbly.

Compliment a woman when she wears nice shoes.

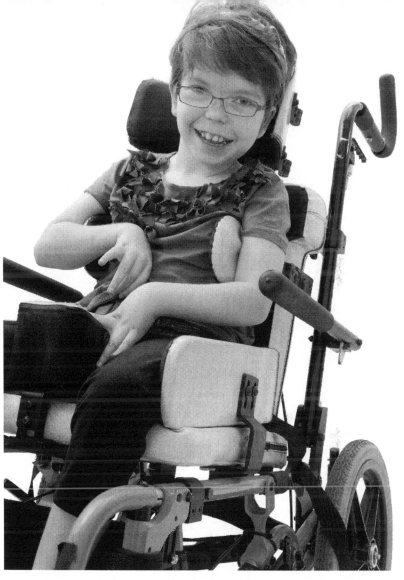

Happiness is a choice. Think about your problems and you'll be sad. Think about your blessings and you'll be happy.

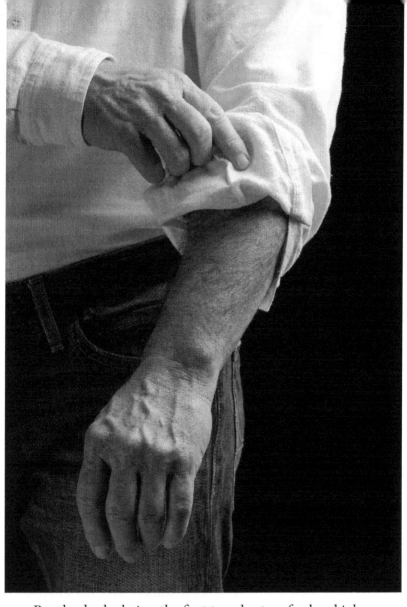

Be a leader by being the first to volunteer for hard jobs.

Keep dating your spouse when you get married.

~

The beauty of a virtuous woman never fades.

~

Save money on insurance by raising your deductible.

~

Imagine how happy you'd be if your problems doubled and then returned to the previous level.

~

Ask questions. People will think you're wise, not ignorant.

When something beautiful captures your attention, stop, gaze, and reflect. Don't move on until it's captured your heart too.

Don't be defensive when someone criticizes you. Examine the criticism to see if you can benefit from it.

~

You won't be happy with what you have until you're happy with who you are.

~

Know your purpose, and the certainty within you will withstand the uncertainty around you.

~

Tell your mother- and father-in-law you love and appreciate them.

~

People who can say no to themselves and others have great power.

~

Your character is measured by how well you do the small things no one sees.

~

The most important day for successful people is today. For failures, it's tomorrow.

A Little Guide to a Big Life

Don't always invite the same people to your parties.

~

Check regularly to see if your daily activities are moving you toward your goals.

~

Don't try to please everyone. It's a full-time job with low pay – and no one has ever succeeded.

~

Improve your relationship with your boss by focusing on what you can do better, not on what he or she can do better.

Hug the person you're forgiving.

~

Don't delay happiness until you're successful. The journey – taking risks, overcoming obstacles, and building relationships – is the best part.

~

Don't blame your financial troubles on your salary. If you doubled your income, you'd probably double your expenses too, and still be short of money. More money isn't the solution. Discipline yourself to live on what you have.

Your most important work is at home.

A demanding boss can be your biggest ally if you do great work.

Show affection to your spouse in front of your children.

Give your children lots of opportunities to play. It'll be some of their most productive time. They'll explore, learn, create, make friends, and overcome obstacles, which will give them the confidence to handle the real issues of life.

Talent sparkles and then fizzles. Hard work is unseen, but it yields a rich harvest.

~

When you struggle to achieve a goal, remind yourself of the reward, such as better health, and then take the next step.

~

Details are the building blocks of greatness.

~

Don't base your self-esteem on what you do. If something stops you from doing it, you'll feel worthless. Instead, base it on who you are.

Memorize a Bible verse that will give you hope when you're discouraged.

Hands are for pats on the back.

~

Don't give your children everything they want. They need a reason to save money.

~

When you face an obstacle, visualize the times you succeeded, not the times you failed.

~

You're not a mistake; you're a miracle. You're not a failure; you're a fighter. And you're not finished; you're stronger and wiser, better equipped to fulfill your purpose.

God gives everyone talents, opportunities, and a calling, and He enables everyone to succeed with their unique combination.

A Little Guide to a Big Life

Be a counselor at a summer camp for foster children.

Be as polite to your spouse as you are to others.

～

If you want to be like Jesus, love the unlovable.

～

Stay calm when people offend you. They're more likely to acknowledge their mistakes if you're humble.

～

Sunsets are for showing you how beautiful the color orange is.

～

Don't try to keep up with the Joneses, especially if they're in debt.

～

Eat like a thin king. Savor your food and eat slowly. You'll eat less and still feel full.

～

It's been said that a farm is what a city man dreams of at 5:00 p.m., never at 5:00 a.m. Every life has problems. Changing jobs or spouses may not be the answer. Success doesn't lie in eliminating trouble, but in learning from it.

Wise people don't show their wisdom by giving advice. They show it by not giving advice, unless they're asked.

~

A great conversationalist brings out the charm in others.

~

Satisfaction with God is the beginning of all satisfaction.

~

Associate with people you want to be like.

~

Don't top someone else's story.

Make your children feel needed.

Lampposts are for swinging around.

~

Parents don't have time to do everything perfectly. When you take a shortcut, don't turn it into a guilt trip, and don't compare yourself to other parents. They don't have time to do everything perfectly either. Relax and stay calm, and you'll raise happy kids.

~

Obstacles may not get smaller, but you can get bigger.

~

You can make decisions faster when you have goals, because you know what you want.

Hunt for treasure every day. Find an interesting person to talk to. Look for something beautiful in nature. Catch someone doing a good deed. Learn a new word. Find something to be thankful for.

You miss a lot of nice moments when you hurry.

~

Help a friend in need before he or she asks.

~

You think you're better than the people you don't forgive.
Avoid pride by forgiving everyone.

People with a good attitude succeed regardless of the circumstances. Low pay, no recognition, unfair treatment, broken promises – it doesn't matter. They persevere and prosper.

～

Successful people spend more time developing their strengths than eliminating their weaknesses.

～

Small acts performed by the unlikeliest people have changed the course of history.

～

A woman who feels beautiful on the inside will take care of herself, dress nicely, and radiate joy, which will make her irresistible.

～

When someone is thirsty, he or she needs water, not gold. Don't despise your talents. Someone needs what you have to give.

～

Ask others for advice or help. They'll think you're wise for asking them.

When life forces you to slow down, take advantage of it. Make a new friend, call an old friend, learn something new, or admire something as if you were seeing it for the first time. Slow times can be fulfilling.

∼

The most effective motivation is internal. You create it by moving toward a goal. Take the first step and you'll motivate yourself.

Drive as if all other vehicles were driven by one of your children.

Be more interested in your spouse than anything else.

If Dr. Seuss had tried to write like Shakespeare, then we wouldn't be able to enjoy Dr. Seuss. Develop your unique talents. Don't imitate someone else.

~

Attitude is the additive that keeps you going when others have given up.

~

An encounter with God is marked by humility.

~

Failures think their destiny is out of their control, so they don't work hard. Successful people control their destiny by working hard.

A Little Guide to a Big Life

The fountain of youth is in your backyard. To feel like a kid, play like a kid. Jump on a trampoline, spin a hula hoop, or run through a sprinkler.

~

Some people prefer the certainty of misery to the misery of uncertainty. If you're afraid you might go from a bad situation to a worse one, consider this: If you change and things get better, you'll be happy. If you change and things get worse, you can change again, and keep changing, until they get better. But if you don't change, your situation will never improve.

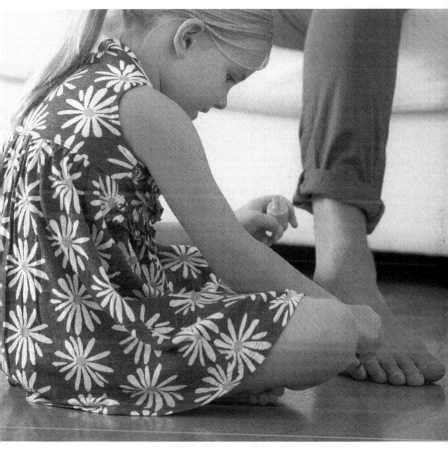

When it comes to your children, spend more time and less money.

~

When misfortune hits, avoid bitterness by focusing on what you can learn from it, the fact that you've been spared many times, and the blessings that remain.

Greet your spouse and children as warmly as your dog greets you.

~

To be happy, absorb yourself in what you're doing at the moment. Resist distractions, such as thoughts about what you're going to do next.

When it comes to money, possessions, fame, and success, the chase is more fun than the catch.

Happiness is a warm hug.

When you're exhausted from taking care of your child, remember that you're not just wiping a runny nose, you're raising someone who may run a university, discover a life-saving drug, or feed the poor.

~

Ask your spouse how you could be a better mate.

~

The road to success is always under construction, so you'll have to take a detour – and the detour may be under construction too. How, then, can you reach your goals? Like all successful people, you persevere with a good attitude, overcoming each obstacle as it comes.

Impress people and they'll soon forget. Impact them and they'll always remember.

Don't let what you don't have keep you from enjoying what you do have.

~

Don't try to impress others with big words.

Take a walk with your children and let them show you the wonders of the world. They'll amaze you with their knowledge.

~

Do what's right in small matters and people will trust you in big matters.

~

Ordinary people in the hands of an extraordinary God can do extraordinary things.

~

Don't hide all of your problems from your children. They learn how to solve theirs by watching you solve yours.

Put a pinwheel in an outdoor flowerpot.

A Little Guide to a Big Life

If you have food to eat, books to read, people to meet, grass to walk barefoot on, and songs to sing, then you have some of the best things in life.

People may forget your good advice, but they won't forget your good example.

~

Forget the faults of others as quickly as you forget your own.

~

Build your confidence by first setting easy goals and achieving them. Then set harder ones.

~

You aren't paid to like your boss, but you are paid to do your best work, regardless of his or her shortcomings.

Don't lower your expectations when life doesn't go as planned. Be bold. Set sail on a new, bigger adventure.

~

Kindness accomplishes more than anger.

~

The most versatile tool is a good attitude. It'll fix anything.

~

When your wife tells you about a problem, don't tell her how to fix it. Just listen and let her know you understand how she feels. She needs your ear, not your advice.

If you constantly criticize your children, they'll feel incompetent and unloved. Correct them when necessary, but find things to compliment too. A good way to eliminate negative behavior is to increase positive behavior, which you can do through praise.

~

The reward for doing your daily duty is happiness.

~

Don't spread yourself too thin by trying to do everything, or you'll be a stranger in your own home.

~

Look up the meaning of unfamiliar words.

A Little Guide to a Big Life

To take hold of the future, let go of the past.

~

Good luck weakens character, if it brings too much leisure. Bad luck strengthens it, if it's met boldly.

~

Success is temporary. The only things that last are the things we do for others.

~

Don't punch holes in anyone's dream. They might surprise you.

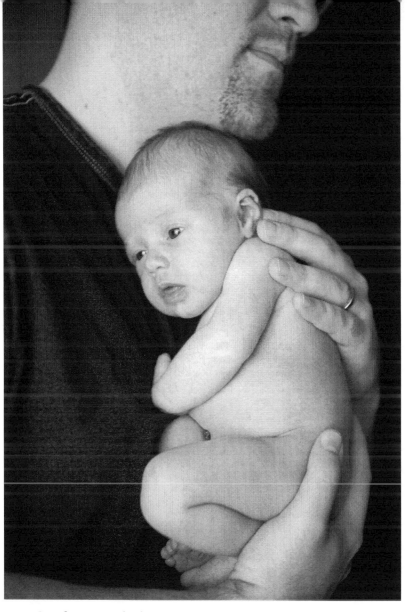

Gentleness melts hearts.

A budget is a plan to have money when other people run out.

Give gifts for no reason.

~

A menial job doesn't have to be a dead end. Many people rose from the bottom to the top because they treated every job like it was the most important one in the world.

~

Read the best books, see the best art, and listen to the best music. You don't have to be rich to enjoy a rich life.

Few great people do big deeds. Most do small deeds in a great way.

If a visually impaired climber can reach the top of Mount Everest, then no obstacle should be too big for people with sight.

A Little Guide to a Big Life

Goals give you a reason to get up in the morning.

Forgiveness lifts a burden off both the forgiven and the forgiver.

You'll have fonder memories of your time with family and friends than of your accomplishments.

~

Meeting people, whether for the first or the thousandth time, is an honor. So light up your eyes, smile, and speak warmly.

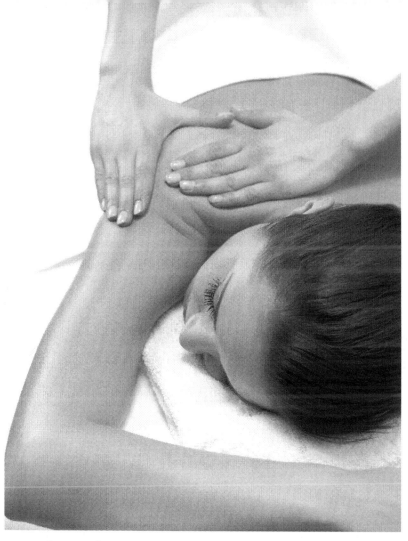

When you're overwhelmed with responsibilities and too busy to take a break, take one anyway. Relax and recharge so you can tackle life's challenges with energy and a good attitude. You'll get more done in less time.

Kids need less care as they grow older, but not less attention.

~

Life is like a round hole. Don't try to fill it with square pegs, such as achievement and wealth. They won't satisfy. Instead, discover your God-given purpose and fulfill it. That's the only way to be happy.

~

Tell your spouse at least once a day how much you appreciate everything he or she does for you and the family, and give an example.

The best part of success is the relationships you develop along the way. Don't hurry or you may mishandle them.

~

Live every moment as if it were the sole purpose of your life.

Dear Friend,

I need your help. If you enjoyed this book, please take a few minutes to post a review on Amazon.com. Your review will help others find this little guide.

Feel free to write me at davidarnoldyoung@gmail.com. I look forward to hearing from you.

Have a big life,
David Young

About the Author

David Young was an advisor to Texas Governor Rick Perry for ten years. He developed the governor's low-cost degree initiative, which challenged universities to offer degrees that cost $10,000. Today, thirteen universities in Texas offer one or more bachelor's degrees for approximately $10,000. This initiative spread to other states, including Florida, where twenty-three institutions offer $10,000 degrees, and to California, which is developing similar low-cost programs.

David enjoys playing the violin and traveling. He; his wife, Christina; and their two dogs live in Round Rock, Texas.

Also by David Young

Breakthrough Power

Breakthrough Power for Mothers

Breakthrough Power for Fathers

Breakthrough Power for Christians

Breakthrough Power for Leaders

Breakthrough Power for Athletes

Breakthrough Power for Golfers

Rebound Strong

Great Funny Quotes